MW00411742

Throw Me A Bone

Poetry For Dogs

and "Shut Up, Artie!"

Artie Isaac

Throw Me A Bone: Poetry For Dogs and "Shut Up, Artie!" include recollections and imagined conversations with real people and dogs. Some names and identifying details have been changed.

Printed on demand via Amazon Kindle Direct Publishing with chlorine-free ink on acid-free interior paper, supplied by a Forest Stewardship Council-certified provider and made from 30% post-consumer waste recycled material.

Front: watercolor painting by Alisa Isaac, based on a photograph by Matt Slaybaugh of Beckett. © 2019 by Alisa Isaac

Back: photograph by Alisa Isaac of Beauregard and Artie in Bexley, Ohio. © 2013 by Alisa Isaac

Written during *Shut Up & Write®: Greene County* at Emporium Wines & The Underdog Cafe in Yellow Springs, Ohio, while drafting an essay, "Canine Poetry Slam," for The 2020 Club, Columbus, Ohio. For more on *Shut Up & Write!*, see shutupwrite.com.

Net proceeds will be donated to Columbus Humane,
the Humane Society of Greene County,
and the Humane Society of the United States.

Artie Isaac will read his poems to you and your friends
for a $2,500 donation to the humane society of your choice.

Adopt, volunteer, contribute, and get help at
columbushumane.org
humanesocietygreenecounty.com
humanesociety.org

*If that dog can find a better deal out there,
he should take it.*

— *Dad*

For Margot

Contents

The Favor

You are sitting, staring, pecking at your desk.

I am on the floor, stretching, beside the ball.

Let me do you a favor, Goodtime.

Come down here, Goodtime.

Throw this ball and I will bring it back to you.
I will give you purpose.
I will return you to here and now.

I will do you the favor of returning you to us.

What We Are Doing Now

You were over there.
I was over there.

Now we are over here.

You can do things I can't do.
I can do things you can't do.

Together, we can do anything.

Dog. Eat. Dog.

Soon after waking,
Foodlady fills the dish.
We eat.

Long into the day,
Foodlady fills the dish.
We eat.

In between, we rely on
Dog.
Eat.
Dog.

Brought in on the wind?
We eat.
Dropped on the floor?
We eat.
Stuck to the wall?
We eat.

In the dish or on the log
Dog.
Eat.
Dog.

Love Of Toys

Toys across the floor,
scattered about.
No tidy pile.

They are work,
in the place of industry,
ready for the next job.

Puppy Love, 1

As I glimpsed you,
I imagined your scent.

You came toward me.
Who are you?
A sniff confirmed:
I love you.

Together.
Urgently, gently.
Hearts leashed
to one another
for life.

Why wouldn't we?

The Door

I fought the door.
I fought the door.
I fought the door.

And the door won.

Cold Surprise

An ice cube in my water dish.
Goodtime's new idea.
Har-dee-barkin'-har.

A Dog Upon Meeting

I see a dog.
I need to get there.
Over there.
Over there.

The force behind me.
Foodlady.
She slows me down.
I pull Foodlady to get to the dog.

Ah, dog! A dog. A dog.
The smell. The smell of the dog.
What a smell.
In my nose I can sense the dog.
The dog comes from food.
The dog comes from shampoo.
The dog comes from an ancient family of dogs.

The dog is a message in a bottle,
washed up on my olfactory shores,
beached in my nose,
held in my heart.

I love the dog.

A Bark In The Night

We heard that?

We did hear that.

We heard that?

It was a bark in the night.
Out across the darkness.
Over the fence, I'm sure.

Big dog.
What does that big dog bark?

Bark! Bark!
I bark in return.
Like throwing the tennis ball back.

Now, quiet.
Waiting.

Kibble

Oh, my dog.
Foodlady.
A bowl of kibble.
Dry crunchies.

With some chicken.

Excuse me. I'm eating.

Do you think I eat fast?
I eat this fast only because
I cannot eat faster.

Good kibble — with chicken —
deserves to be eaten quickly.

Jim Rides His Bicycle

That man has wheels.
He flies.

He smiles as he flies.
His hands are in the air.
The wheels turn.

He flies as fast as big dogs run.

I will run with him.

Hurry, Goodtime!
The man is flying past.

Uncertainty Principle

Where to pee is a wonder.
Not here. Here.
Not here. Here.

I do not know where to pee.
But I do know when.

When to pee?
Right now.

Call Me By My Name

You call me "Margo."
You call me "Gogo."
You call me "DogDog."
You call me "Pooch."
You call me "Little Buddy."

I think my name is "Clark."
Because that is what other dogs say when they see me.

"Clark!" "Clark!"

What The Bark?

What is it with you?

You want me to sit.
You want me to lie down.
You want me to speak.
You want me to stay.
You want me to roll over
and play dead.

Play dead?
There's something disturbing about that one.

My life is shorter than yours.
One of your years equal to seven of mine.

You can have seven dogs.
I get only one of you.

Unless both of us is truly unlucky.
You would be unlucky to be untimely dead.
I would be unlucky because you are Foodlady in life.
In death? You might only be food.

Are you sitting down?
My playing dead is just a vision of our future.

We won't be playing then.

Running Before Bed

After your bath, you step on the scale.
Before my crate, I want to run about.

Here.
Now here.
Now here.

I can see everything at once.
I am our night watchman,
making my final rounds,
checking on everything,
speedily as I can.

I sleep best right after I run about.
A tired dog is a happy dog.

Go figure.

You should try it.

Maybe you would not toss and turn all night,
if the last thing you saw was not your weight.

Thank You For Your Service

Where you have been all day?
I wag your return.
You bring home the kibble.

And you pick up my poop.
(Strange pleasure of yours.
Whatever. Take what you want.)

I'm glad you work for me.
You are a service human.

Wait! Wait! Wait!

Walks are for smelling.

I have to check my p-mail.
On my pole.
On my rock.
On my low hanging magnolia leaf.
As my black nose dances a half breath away,
I am like a detective, dusting for fingerprints.

I've got p-mail.

Reply all!

Tail

You lurk behind me.

I will get you, wispy nemesis.

I am coming for you.

I will get you.

Ha HA!

(Harrumph.)

Wake up. Now.

I'm barking in the dark,
splitting the night
and your sleep.

Because I love you.

Because we are not safe here.

I smell storm.
A big one.
I am barking:
wake and comprehend.

Let's get up. Now.
We need stronger shelter.
Somewhere safer.

Forgive me for waking you
with ten minutes to spare.
You could have slept
a little longer.

But, now, the last moments of calm,
there's time to go out front for a pee.

Then, in the basement,
on that old couch,
we will softly sing hymns
and snuggle for safety
and love.

My Puppy Neck

I cannot turn my head slowly.
I have to look here
— and here
— and here.

My head moves so quickly.
From here
— to here
— to here.

So quickly that I do not know
that here
— is near here
— is near here.

Rain

Out?
Now?
No.
Rain.
Later.

Now?
No.
Rain.
Later.

Shoe

A shoe!

What fun.
Strings and leather.
Small enough to drag.
Light enough to shake.
Good chew.
Friendly smell:
Goodtime!

I'll take one.
You can have the other.

A Dog Afar

I'm not known for my depth perception.
That's why I crashed into the leg of the dining table
while chasing the ball.

I am looking across the street at a dog.
Is this dog my size?
Is this dog smaller?
Is this dog bigger?

I have no idea.

So I will bark carefree.
And when we are together,
I will face the truth.

How bad can it be?

Chimera

Something rich happened here
on the middle of the road.
It cannot be seen anymore.

Was it dropped by a bird?
Then pressed by a tire?
Then cooked by the sun?

A ghost of what it was,
having lost none of its rich story,
this canine hologram of
a fire-breathing monster.

With Charlie In The Sunshine

We cuddled on the carpet
beside the front window,
warmed by the sun,
both of us curled like commas,
you in 10-point type,
I in 24 points.

I was a boy.
You were fully grown.
We slept in the sun.

I woke, chilled and alone.
The sun had moved on and so had you.
The bath of sun had long emptied.

I got up, looked around,
ready to explain why I was alone
on the dining room floor.

No one was there.
No one ever asked.
I never told anyone.
Until you.
Now.

Beauregard

You survived three:
my mother, her brother, and
a previous owner unknown.
All three claimed to own you
— all of them now scattered
in the grasses to be sniffed by dogs.

Now, my inheritance of fur,
you come to our home.
You are resilient.
You outlived three masters.

I wish you a long life here.
I offer our love, our food, our tennis ball.

But know this:
I will cherish your ashes.

The Dog Deal

Would I take the deal if offered?
I would be fed on a schedule,
the same kibble twice a day
— and never do the dishes.

I could wee-wee at will,
especially out of doors,
and, during bad weather,
slink behind the sofa,
where my scat would never be discovered
— and never clean the bathroom.

I could nap in the sun by the door,
and move to the other side of the house,
following the sun,
to nap beside the window
— and never go to work.

I could prance around in my howdy-hoo
— and never do laundry.

I would be split from my siblings forever.
My parents would not witness my growth.
I would arrive a stranger in a strange home.

I would turn three magic circles
and sleep right there.

What would become of me?
Would my ambitions atrophy?
Would my etiquette evaporate?

Or would I rise to the Divine,
— a creature of life, of love?

Not Much, But Now

Our needs are few,
But they are now.

Never later.

When it is time to play ball,
that time is now.

The Butterfly and The Bee

You both dance in the air
above my head.
I leap to meet you.
I long to close you in my mouth.

You, butterfly, you are tissue in the air.
You, bee, you are a floating fuzzy.

I have not yet.
But I will.

Puppy Love, 2

Big decisions happen all at once
over a long period of time.

You were no longer a puppy.
Your wild moves had bloomed into adulthood.

But suddenly,
your adulthood had wilted into frailty.

I asked the doctor on the phone
an hour ago, late that night.

"Will he run again?"

"No," the quiet reply.

Now we are sitting on this black vinyl couch.
Foodlady, you, and me.
I've been your Goodtime.
But I don't feel like Goodtime now.

I look down at you,
swaddled in the veterinarian's blanket.

I don't know what to say.
What comes to my lips
is what I have always thought of you.

"Good dog."
My voice cracks.

You hear the name you earned: Gooddog.
You look up, with your abiding love.
I look down, realizing our life of love.

We all look at the vet.
I nod.

You rest your head
and close your eyes.

The vet — a kindly soul —
says, "That was for sleep.

"This will stop the heart."

With a great sigh, you are gone.

*****

Whenever I need to cry
(I do need to cry),
I think of that moment you looked up
when you heard, "Good dog."
My eyes fill with tears. I cry.

This is the last trick you taught me,
Gooddog:
how to make the two-foot drop
from my head to my heart
and back to my eyes filling with tears,
this moment, to my own heart's stop.

Sleeping Breath

We are together in the dark.

I hear your breathing
in your sleep.

Soon, you will hear
my sleeping breath.

We take turns
sleeping breath.

Artie, shut up!
from *Net Cotton Content*

After my sisters had all left the house as adults, my parents and I ate dinner around the little kitchen table.

I don't think emotion played much of a role in that decision. No one wept, "Oh, we can't eat at the big dining room table without those wonderful girls."

We soon forgot that they ever lived with us. It was cleaner that way.

We moved into the kitchen for ease. I mean, shoot: the stove is right there. The refrigerator is right *there*. If the kitchen were any smaller, we wouldn't have to serve the food at all. I could just lean back and grab the cottage cheese out of the fridge. Mom could reach with the big spoon into the succotash on the stove top.

It was sweet.

Without my sisters as role models at the table stunting me with a little encouragement, I quickly became one of the adults. That was wise: growing up in my house there weren't children; there were only little adults.

I began my life as an only child at that table.

It was handy to be an only child. That's how I learned stand-up comedy.

I learned it in two parts. Whenever I'd finished my dinner, I'd stand up. (That's the first part.) Then I would stand beside the table and ask to be excused. Because my request was denied, I would stand by and entertain them. They would laugh. Everyone got something out of the deal.

**But this is a story
about our dog …**

… and his allergies.

Charlie was a complex West Highland White Terrier. He was seriously allergic to sun, air and grass. For a dog, this is the definition of inconvenience. Naturally, when we placed him out on the dog line in the back yard, he would bark incessantly at his nemeses.

Because our house was not big on emotional intelligence, no one wondered whether the dog was dying from his allergies. We figured that he was barking at the squirrels. We thought his barking was a lifestyle choice.

Unfortunately, for Charlie, there could be no dogs in our house, only little adults. So he was constantly told not to do things that Mother Nature required him to do. Bark. Lick people, his genitals, people, his genitals. Bark.

We should have just named him "Don't bark." Or "Don't lick." It would have saved a lot of time.

Barking was not considered Charlie's native talent. It was considered a curse on the neighbors. How could they live peacefully when our dog is barking? For the sake of the neighbors, we would plead with him, "Don't bark." He still barked, but at least the neighbors might hear our scolding and know that we cared about keeping the peace in the neighborhood.

So, really, now, this is a story about one specific dinner.

There we were: Dad (also "Artie"), Mom, Little Artie at the table. Charlie on his line, barking his head off as he slowly twists in the wind, sun, and grass.

Having heard quite enough from the dog, my mom shakes her head and gets up from the table. She walks to the screen door and shouts with determination into the yard (and beyond):

"Artie, shut up!"

My father and I glance at each other. As the only males, neutered or otherwise, named "Artie" on the estate, we recognized our name. She'd yelled, "*Artie*, shut up!"

My dad stopped chewing and slowly shook his head.

Mom returned to the table, the color drained from her face. She looked at us and quietly asked, "I did it, didn't I?" She already knew. We nodded.

I couldn't see Charlie, so I don't know what he did. He was definitely quiet. He knew his name was a word like "Charlie" or something to do with licking and barking. I can still imagine him in the backyard, stunned into silence, holding his head at The Angle Of Dog Confusion, and figuring that the family was finally on the rocks.

The same, no doubt, occurred to the neighbors. The Iannaris next door surely heard my mother's shout. Someone must have looked up from *their* dinner and said, "The Isaacs always seemed so happy. Huh."

from *artie.co*
December 31, 2007

Thank you.

Thank you, beloved Alisa, for your artistic contributions, for changing "Bigstink" to "Goodtime," and for being our Foodlady.

I am grateful that:

— Adam Harris observed that I am drawn to every dog
— Matt Slaybaugh taught me *The Absurdity Of Writing Poetry*
— Beth Weinstock edited these poems with skill and care
— Johnrick Hole edited and audited for originality
— K. Srikrishna invited me to *Shut Up & Write*
— *Creativity & Personal Mastery* sparked greater mindfulness
— Judi Allen and Sean Allen lovingly delivered Margot
— Jackie Isaac took in two Charlies, Casey, and Beauregard
— thousands of strangers let me greet their dogs.

June 30, 2019
Yellow Springs, Ohio

More Poetry For Dogs!

Next: dog-friendly poems from readers of *Throw Me A Bone*.

For consideration, send your poem to artieisaac@gmail.com.

From *Throw Us More Bones…*

Wait For Me
(Ode To Sassy)

by Mike Jenkins

Wait for me.
I will be back soon.
Sleep sound in that truth.

Drink some water.
Avoid the trash;
It is not for you.
Listen for my return.
It may be a surprise,
Or maybe you will see me
From your window perch.
I will be excited to see you,
And you, me. I can't wait to
Scratch your ears and head
Rub your belly and
Hold you once again.
Take you for a nice long walk.
Until you pull me home again.

Wait for me.
I will be back soon.
Because of you.
For you.
For me.

Throw Us
More Bones

More Poetry For Dogs

Artie Isaac, editor

© 2019, Mike Jenkins. Mike Jenkins lives in Michigan with Jan, and enjoys time with Chicago granddog Sassy.

Made in the USA
Monee, IL
03 September 2019